LETTER FROM THE EDITORS

     We as YOUNG IGNORANTES like to break down walls that our families might be too scared or embarrassed to take a sledge hammer to. Our generation has awoken in the midst of a consuming fog that people before us have ignored. We are addicted to the warmth that the sun bestows on us when it can break through the mist and we aren't going to be silent about needing it to shine down on us more than it does now.

     In this issue, IN SICKNESS, we have opened up and shown our most vulnerable selves. We are no longer hiding the anxiety that can take control of our daily lives or the depression that threatens to break us. Mental illness has always been here and will always be here and we refuse to keep ignoring it. We're going to openly talk about it, we're going to help each other find pockets of calms in each other's storms and we're going to create a culture of offering a shoulder to cry on or lending a kind ear. We're taking care of ourselves and writing down these unwanted emotions that have taken control over our lives. No longer can we continue the cycle of refusing to name our demons and ignoring the burdens that threaten our very lives everyday. We are naming them and facing them head on.

     With our poems, photographs and stories, we fight against this undesired pain. We hope that with these works, you'll know that you aren't alone in this battle. We are here with you and we won't let you go. We hope that you feel the sun's warmth while you read this issue, that you find the light among the fog and run. It's alright to feel what you feel and take a break, but don't give up. We are all rooting for you, we are all breaking down this wall and searching for the sun. We won't give up on you.

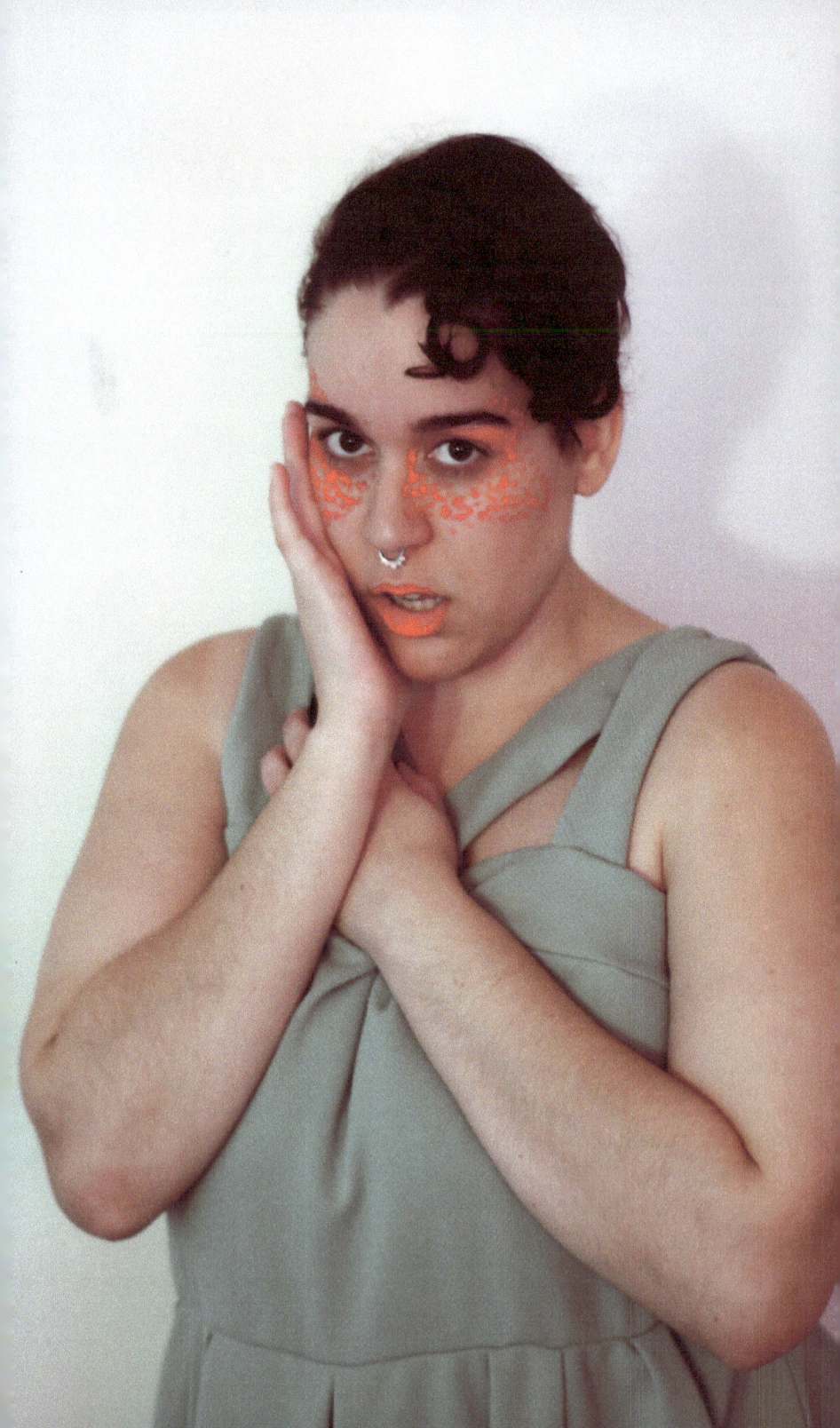

THIS MONTH

- 5   THE ONLY CURE
- 9   LOVE POEMS FOR HEALING
- 11 FOGGY WALL
- 13 WHY I WRITE
- 14 IT HURTS TO STAND STILL
- 16 I WANT A DIVORCE
- 17 TIME IS NOT LINEAR
- 20 THIEF
- 22 VANITY
- 23 EMPTY

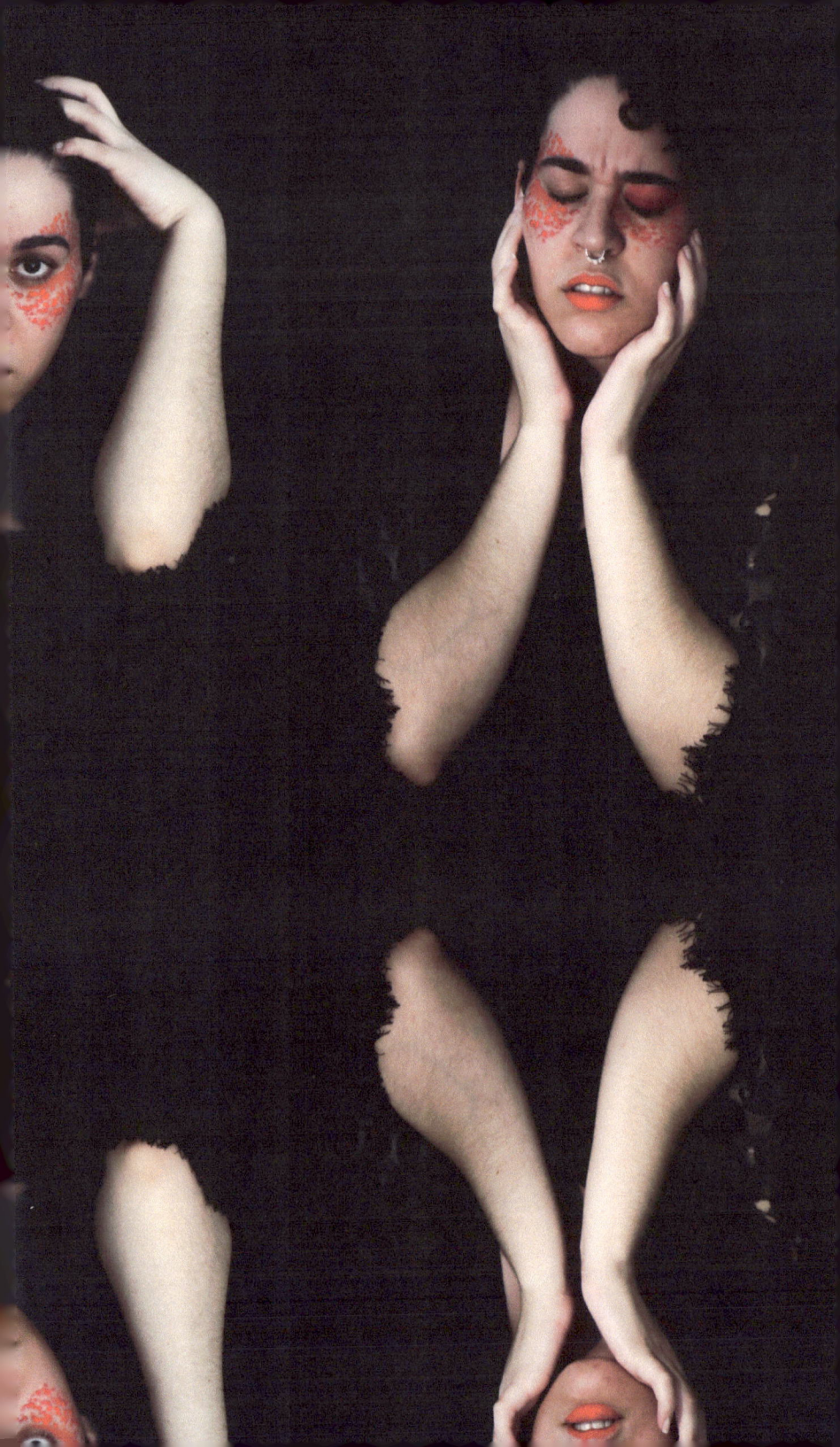

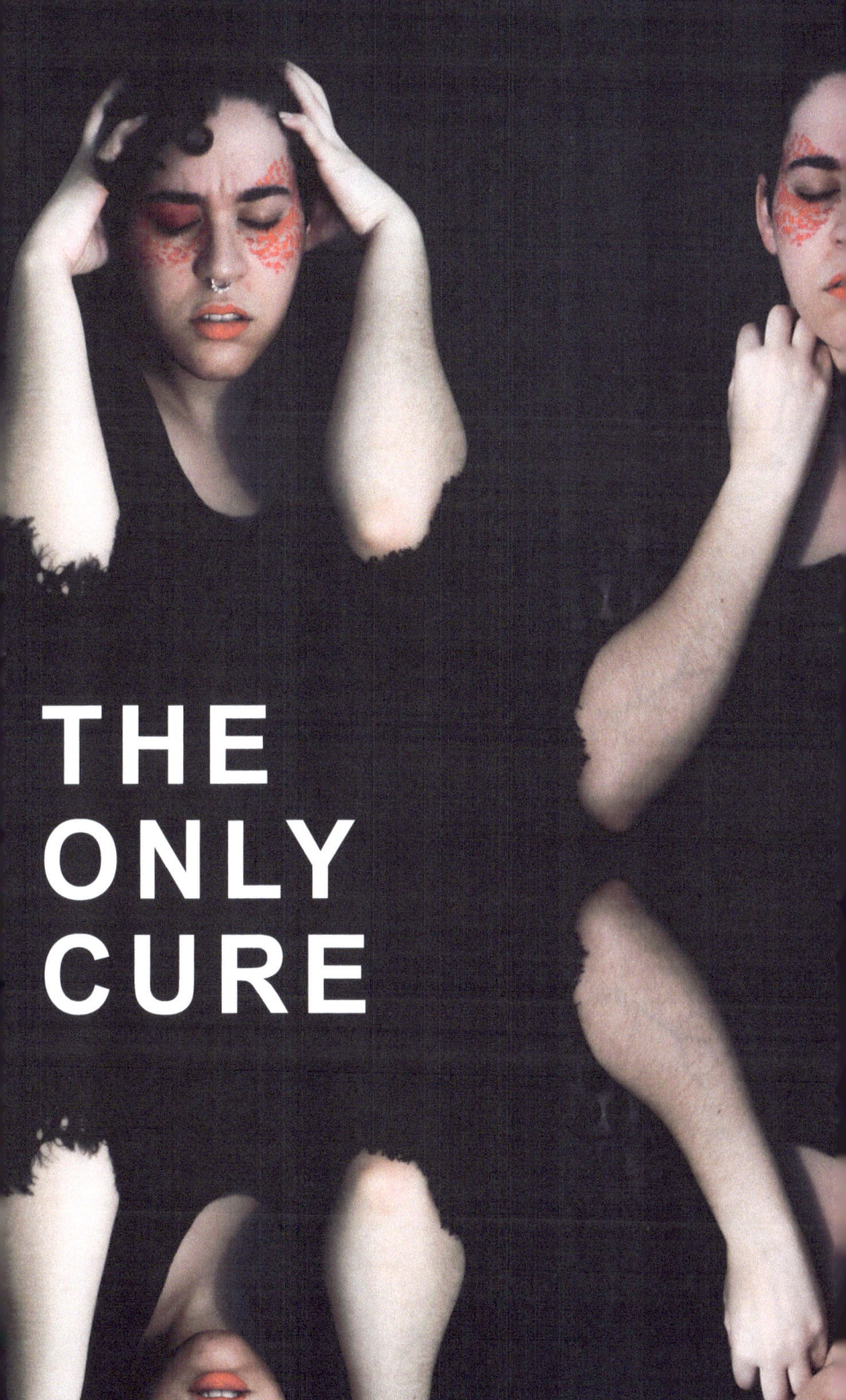

JOSEPHINE JAEL JIMENEZ

We were in the car, my mother, my sister and I. My mother started talking about someone I love and how poorly their life had turned out because they decided not to follow the Lord the way she had. It's the same thing I've heard over and over again throughout my life, but then she started talking about how sad they were sometimes.

"Her depression never goes away because she doesn't follow the Lord. That's the only cure." It sounded better in Spanish, kinder almost, but that's how they get you down in my grandma's village. They make ignorance sound so sweet.

My mother and I used to fight all the time, mostly because I was never the kind of kid she wanted. I was never the sheep that blindly followed the shepherd or the kind that went with the other sheep. She was the kind of shepherd that demanded that.

We would fight about cleaning my room mostly, but as I grew up, we started to fight about religion a lot. My parents aren't the type of people that ask too many questions. If the book says to do something and the guy at the pulpit give it the thumbs up, then who am I to question that? Well, I'm the type of person that asks too many questions, according to my dad. He says I've just gotta have faith, I say I like tattoos.

The fights that hurt me the most were always the ones about my depression. I can't tell you how many times I've been told that if I truly loved God, if I truly believed he was real and good, then He would take my depression away. All I had to do was ask. I spent a lot of time asking God to make me happy, to take away the demons in my head, but He never did. For years and years, I thought I wasn't good enough to be healed, cured of my sadness. I thought maybe it was because I didn't like to kneel, it hurt my knees too much. As I got older, I thought it was because I didn't clean my room like my mom said. But then when I grew up, I realized that I didn't need to be cured of depression, I needed to be cured of my expectations and of the image of a God that would choose to leave my brain broken. The cure came after that thought crossed my mind and I found a God that held my hand through the pain and the fog. We all suffer, She would say, and you are no exception. You are not so special that you would be exempt from pain. It's the same song she's been trying to get me to sing all along.

I didn't like that at first. It made me angry because I couldn't see that I was being selfish and stupid. But I was constantly reminded that other people suffer worse. Would I prefer their suffering?

It was never supposed to be about praying away the illness in my brain, it was about allowing the pain to make you really enjoy the times it's not there. Joy and happiness are sweeter now. There are no highs without lows. Life can't be beautiful if it is not also disgusting sometimes. It's about balance.

My mom went on and on in the car about my loved one's kids and the lives they chose to lead, judging the success and the happiness that they found for themselves because it didn't look good to her. She blamed that on not following

God her way, too. Normally, I would have blown up and yelled up to high heaven about depression and fate and how you can't control your kids, but I was tired. I was tired from all the years of having to find peace with God despite the painting of Her my parents had created and hung over the mantel that was my life. I was tired from painting over the image of someone they should have taught me to see the right way in the first place. I was tired from trying to convince them that my painting was also beautiful because it taught me how to see the beauty and majesty in life. But then she said something awful.

"People with depression kill themselves because they didn't have the sense to ask God for help." This is when I spoke up, when my God whispered in my ear to offer a different perspective, that's all I needed to do. So I told my mother she was wrong, again. I told her of the fleeting thoughts in my deepest valleys of how I could get rid of my pain, how easy it was in certain seconds of my life to think of crossing that thin line. It wasn't about loving God, because I do, it was about seeking help and dealing with the fact that I was a little bit broken, that my brain didn't work the way it was supposed to and that it had nothing to do with how many times I prayed. She stopped talking soon after, I think the realization got to her. Once your kid tells you they've thought about trying to meet God, something starts to click.

The conversation left me wishing that these conversations didn't need to keep happening, that maybe one day I wouldn't have to fight for the validity of my ailment. I wish I didn't have to write a whole dissertation style speech every time someone told me it was all in my head or to just do things that make me happy or to just pray the sad away. Maybe one day we'll get there, but for now it's my cross to bear. But who am I to think I'm too special to do it?

EDITORIAL SHOOT
Photographer: Josephine Jael Jimenez
Model: Rebekah C. Guerra

flowers have grown
where my brain and heart
used to be
and while you'd think
this is a good thing
the unforunate part
is that the flowers
may never die

so you tell me
where is
the beauty
in that.

a poem by Sadie Kendrick

LOVE POEMS FOR HEALING

YURA SAPI

Today
I am immensely grateful
for my capacity to love
So
deeply

Love
For others
For self
For life
For changing the world
For making decisions around love

I've realized that because I can love
So
intensely

I also have the capacity
to feel the opposite

Because how could I know
the incredibleness of feeling such a deep love
Without knowing what it's like to not have it

Today I am immensely grateful for my capacity to love.

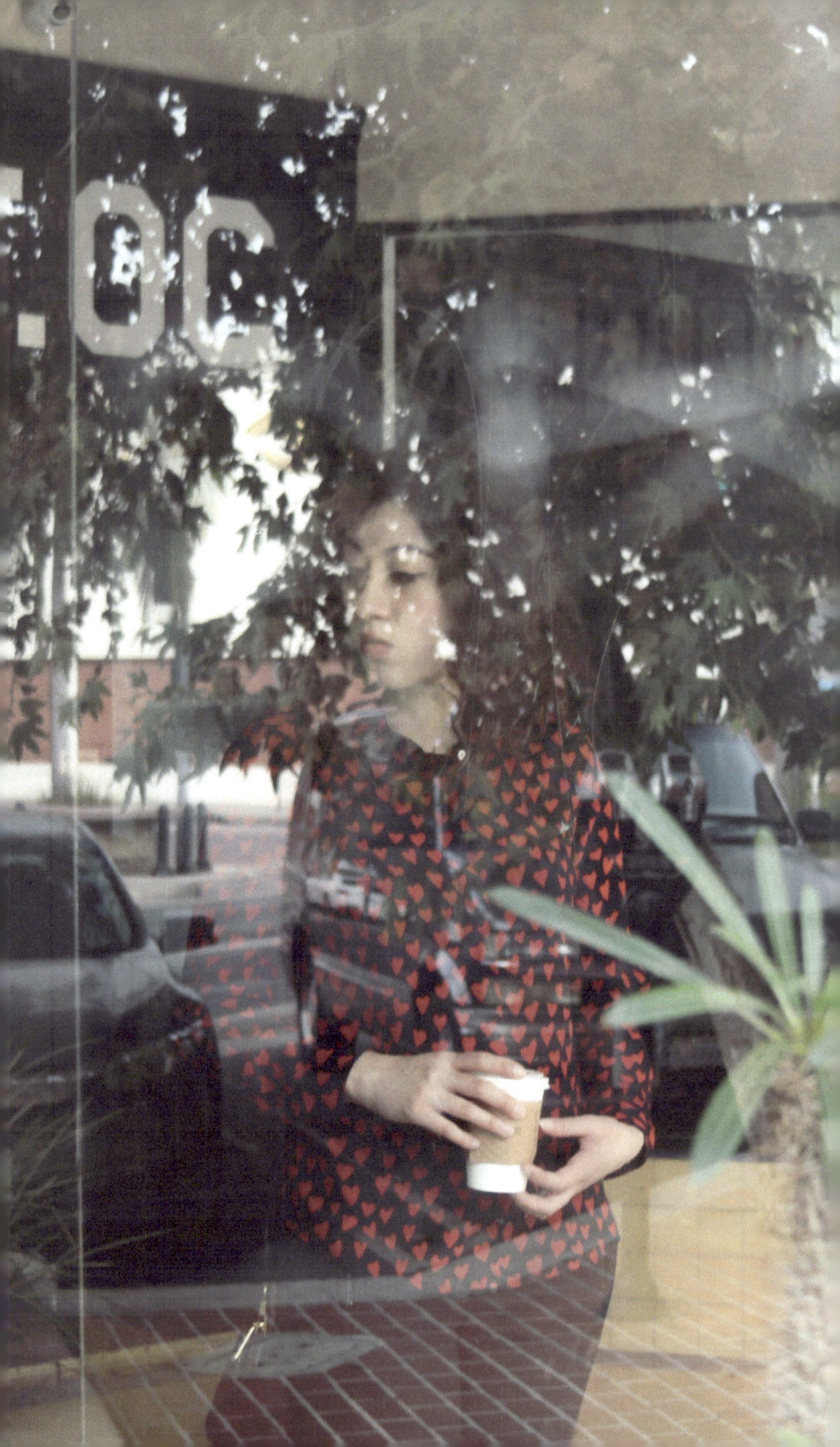

FOGGY WALL

BRENDA HERNÁNDEZ JAIMES

I've been trained to repress any shadow of sadness that threatens to crumble my strength. This destructive advice came from a loved one that didn't want to see my mother suffer from my sadness.

These years of training created a cloud over me and a wall that covers my true emotions. Fear of showing any negative emotion quickly threw me into a black hole.

The consequence of this was for me to suffer in silence and leave me with deep cracks of anger, frustration, and misery. I didn't have the privilege to wallow buried in my bed. My parent's hard work was a powerful motivation to get up every day, place a smile on my face and to continue with my life as if nothing wrong was bubbling inside of me.

Unfortunately, I quickly crumbled alone. I felt fear and shame to show any negative emotions to those who were close to me. Over the years, the cloud became a wall, reinforcing this destructive cycle of drowning in my depression.

But then the person who has loved me the most saved me. With patience and with much effort my mother has helped me break down this wall. To let myself feel and express myself if I feel lost with no explanation. I've taken that deep breath and I've become addicted to it. I want to escape from this fog that has reigned in my life and will most likely continue to be present. But with her support, I know the sun will shine, I will feel its warmth, and the drive to be accepting of myself and my feelings.

For my own mother has suffered from this, but I've also inherited her strength and hunger to live. I know I'll be okay and that's it's okay to stay in bed, for the sun will shine tomorrow and I'll be ready to take on the day.

Photograph *by Josephine Jael Jimenez*

I wonder
if I could see
the scars on my heart
like I can see

the one on my hand from touching the top of the oven

the one on my neck from a sleepy mismotion with the curling iron

the one of my knee from where my ligaments were stitched back together

I wonder
if I could see
if maybe then
I would be more careful with it

about who I lend it to

who I show it to

who I allow to call it home

and
I wonder
if you could see
the scars on my heart
if you'd be more careful with it
too

a poem by Sadie Kendrick

WHY I WRITE

MELISSA ARELLANO

To ask why I write
Is to ask the bird why it flies.
Only in prose
could the image of a single rose,
Be made more beautiful and majestic,
Or the shadow of a single flower
be made more sinister
By the hour.
Molding uncertainties of the heart
Into tear-wrenching works of art.
Uncharted feelings
Chasing, trapping thoughts in a sea
of happiness and misery
To be fabricated and elaborated
to a hungry ear.
Why do I write?
To tell a tale of my own design,
To share the feelings that are only mine,
Or simply because I love to rhyme.

IT HURTS TO STAND STILL

LORRAINE RUMSON

I don't know how I can relax the grip
you have on me. You squeeze me at my heart
'til blood runs through your fingers, down my chest
and burns an acid crater through my stomach.
I want to take a rope to both my wrists
and twist it up until my skin is raw.

I can't spit out the words I need when raw
frustration ties me in a steel-twine grip.
I pound my fists against my prison, wrists
slashed on the rough cell walls, until my heart
beats fast, like when I run. My traitor stomach
heaves up its contents, throws them down my chest.

My dresses are so tight around my chest
I can't lift up my arms. They scrape me raw
until seam-lines have gouged open my stomach
and I'm immobile, paralyzed in their grip.
There has to be some purpose, my sweet heart
lies. I can't feel my hands beyond my wrists.

I feel your absence: heart, throat, belly, wrists,
like you're a great raw wound clawed into my chest
that someone reached through to pull my heart
and all its arteries, snatched from the raw
and gaping cavern; a sadistic grip
has performed surgery against my stomach.

I feel it like a boulder in my stomach.
I reach into the gore up to my wrists
and twist my innards back together, grip
too tightly, cut the blood off from my chest.
Scattered on the floor, I leave raw
meat. My liver, intestines, my heart.

I want to drive a stake into my heart.
I want to take a bread knife to my stomach.
I want to choke myself until the raw
skin splits. I want to break my birdy wrists.
I want to beat on your unwavering chest
as if that could make you relax your grip.

But raw rage never helped an aching heart
release its grip on life. I fear my stomach's
too weak for bloody wrists, or open chests.

I WANT A DIVORCE

ANONYMOUS

I didn't realize I was born in the valley of the shadow of Death

Full of hope in a place that lost all hope
Full of imagination in a place that couldn't look past its own nose
Full of joy in a place that was vehemently abused

The carried trauma is weighing me down
I only wish it could be 6 feet deep
I'm so far into the ground
The Earth's core has swallowed me into its burning hot flame

The screams are no longer fulfilling
The physical exertion is no longer feasible
The tears have dried up

SET ME FREE, MOTHERFUCKER

Let go of my broken heart
My traumatized soul
My tearful eyes

Let me be me
Let me exist with comfort
Let me embrace myself with unconditional love
Let me feel like I can get through a day without wanting to throw myself in front of a train or car
Let me fucking be

TIME IS NOT LINEAR

YURA SAPI

You are not alone
You were never alone
We've been through this cycle before
We're working from the power
Of our past fighters from before
And Time isn't linear
Connections happen for a reason
There's a reason I am here where I am
So bask
Indulge
Refuge
In the happenings of now
The happenings of past
Which will guide to future
Which is also really the past

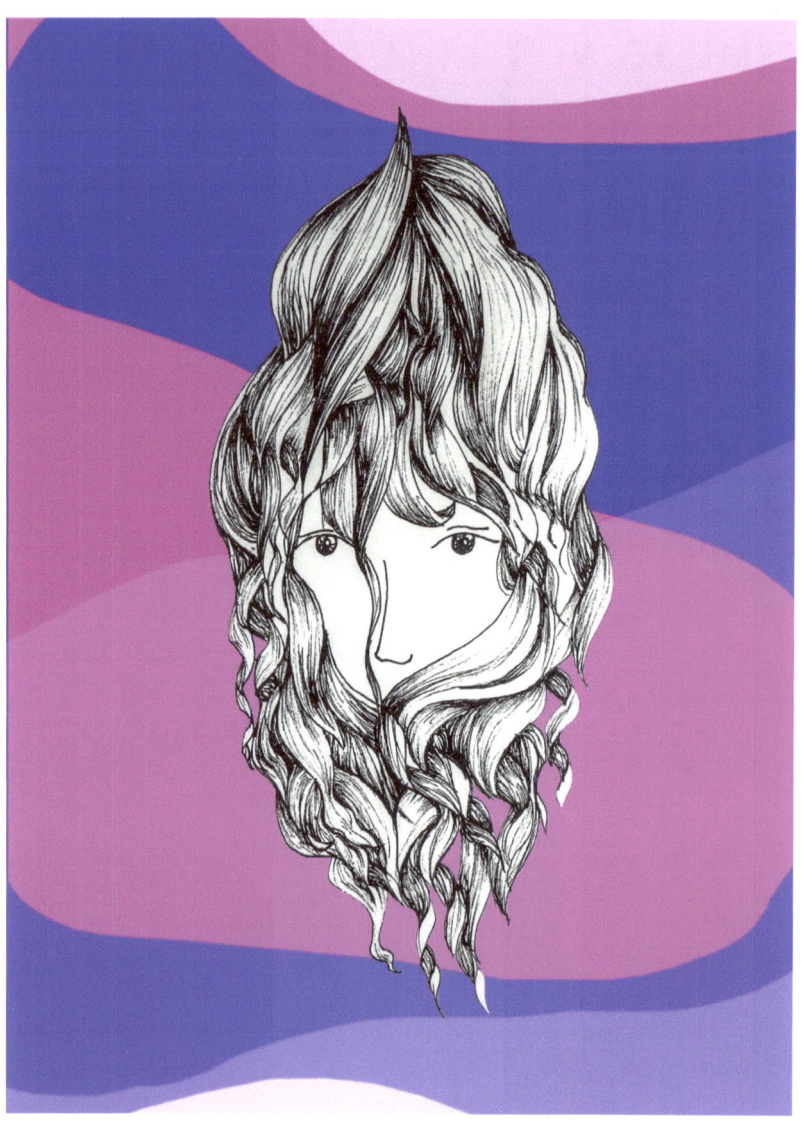

Illustration *by Bekah Badilla*

my defeat
is not young
although it seems freshly grown
adapting to its new skin
familiarizing itself with surroundings
upon its sudden birth

my defeat
is seasoned in its age
through multiple efforts and trials and changes
all withering it down
slowly but surely
breaking it down to the fundamental grain
until it stands naked
in its rawest form
its most organic elements
stripped to its last line

my defeat
holds true there
frozen in time
as suddenly realizing
that the point has been reached
where all that is known
is that
defeat itself

is defeated

a poem by Sadie Kendrick

THIEF
DONYA AVERY

I don't know who I am.
Wait, that's a boring start. Let's go again.
I am a thief.
I have stitched myself an identity out of the scraps of others. I spent my childhood in every world but the real one. In the real world, people hurt me, lied to me, abused me. In the world of fantasy, though, I was safe. I could slip between the lines like a shadow and make myself safe beneath the words. It was escapism of the purest form. Even well into my twenties, I still return to those old haunts, still run my peeling fingers along the walls of memory.
It was safety.
It was also a terrible method of self-discovery.
It took me until 18 to realize that something was wrong. I spent so long hiding, I forgot to resurface. There was no 'me' left. I had dissolved into the pages and left behind a perfectly believable girl-shaped shell. It was an earth-shattering realization. They say our youth is spent journeying head-first into the self. No big deal, right? Just go out there, seize the day, discover the you you've always wanted to be!
Except.
Except there was no foundation. There was nothing but a penchant for daydreaming and an extremely overactive imagination.
So I did the only thing I could think of; I stole. If I draped myself in interesting fabrics and fascinating threads, no one would know I was hollow inside. Like any good forgery I could be intriguing and believable but with the capacity to crumble upon closer inspection.

I met a girl, she had fantastic humor. I took it from her while she was attempting to be my friend. I met a boy, he loved video games. The next day, I loved video games and don't you remember? I've always loved video games. This girl on the internet, she weaved her own beautiful worlds of fantasy. At 3 am I feverishly began a novel I haven't touched in two years. Oh Donya, you're so funny. You're so interesting. You're so self-assured. What a fantastic lie I've built for myself. It's so believable, you see, that I often forget it's as tangible as my letter to Hogwarts.

It took me until 24 to realize this was a mental illness. I spent so long surviving, so long stealing, so long lying, I forgot to ask myself why. Why was I doing this? Was anyone else doing this? Was this just what I would be? A thief. A person-shape fabricated out of lies.

Was the only real thing about me a sickness I don't remember taking?

I'm only two years older and I still don't have solid answers to those questions. Even now, when someone asks me about myself, I give them a detailed list of all my perfectly curated, just-obscure-enough interests to be the version of myself that I am wearing that day. It's my new safe, my new form of escapism.

Maybe one day I'll get better. Maybe one day I'll finally steal the right trait and it will click so perfectly into place that I can stop because I will be whole. Because I will be a real boy. Because I will be normal.

And if not, I'll always have the only thing I ever came by honestly: theft.

VANITY

MELISSA ARELLANO

It's a screaming insanity
This overwhelming vanity
That clouds the mind,
Glitz and glamour
To erase your pallor.
Masks to hide
Writhing feelings lurking inside
That you have had no choice but to hide
What for or why?
Since no one could care less
If you lived or died

EMPTY

YURA SAPI

Hurt
Confused
Bruised
Trying to diffuse
So much being used
So much being
Living
Humanity in all its shades
The pain makes you full
The feelings make you real
The song is salvation
The story is so clear
Time to breathe
Time to process
Good vibes can't always be there
Sometimes the bad has to exist
Everything was the way it was supposed to be
You are enough
You have enough
Yupaychan

We're doing better now
than ever before
and I'll be damned
if I let you take that away.

Evan Black

and then I realized
I find it almost humorous
how long and how hard it takes
to build something up
and how quick and simple it is
to see it break

a poem by Sadie Kendrick

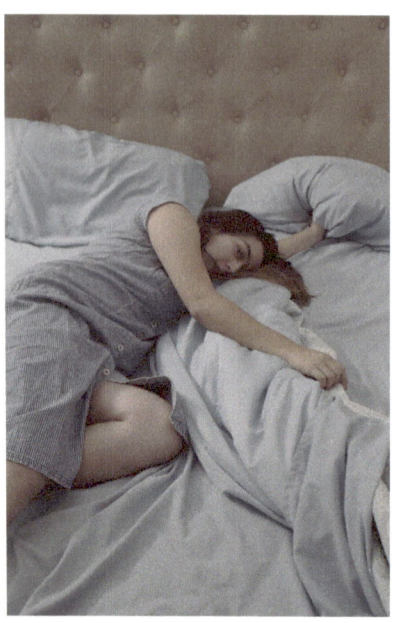
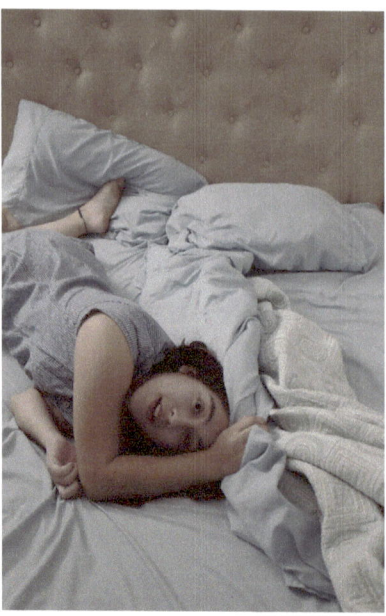
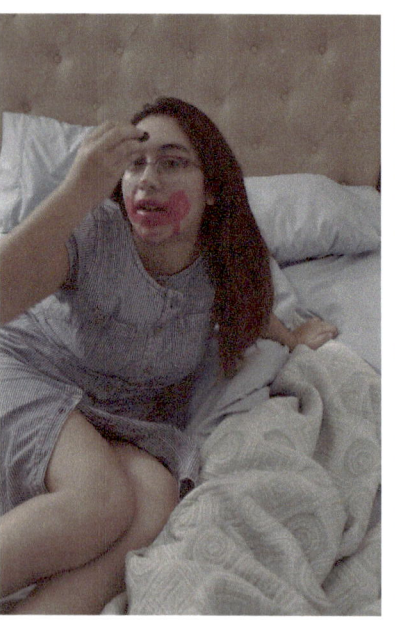
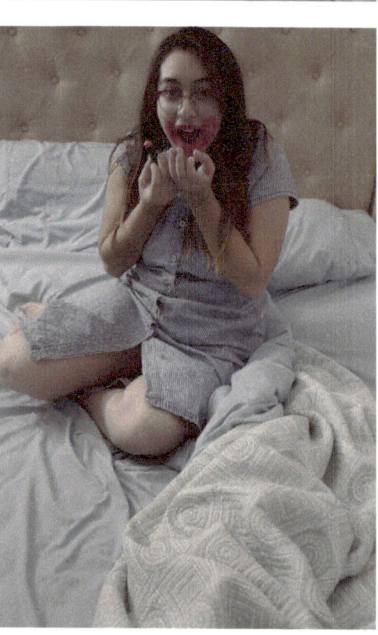

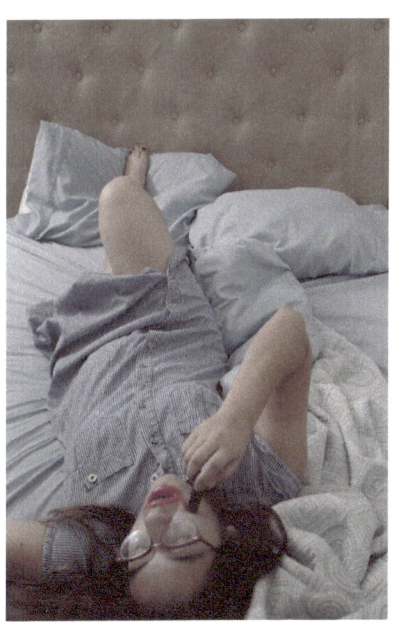
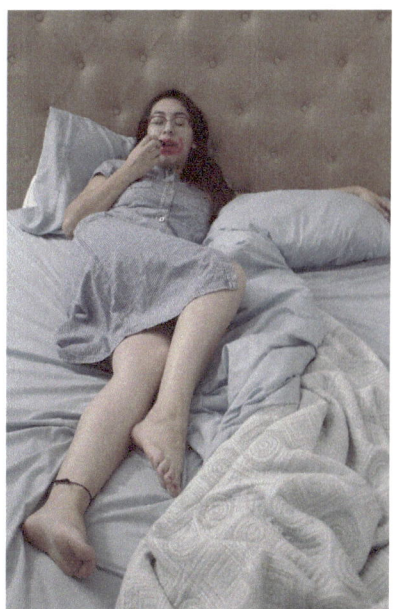
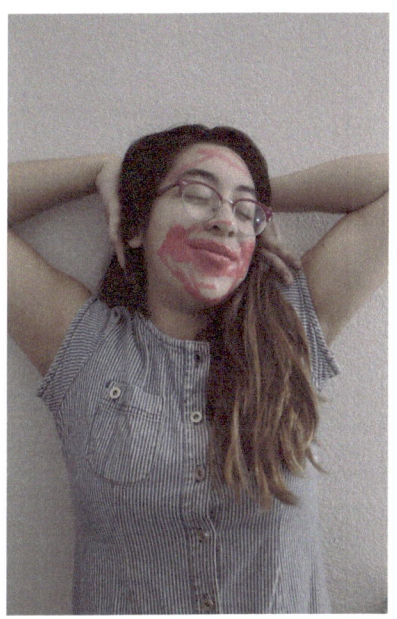
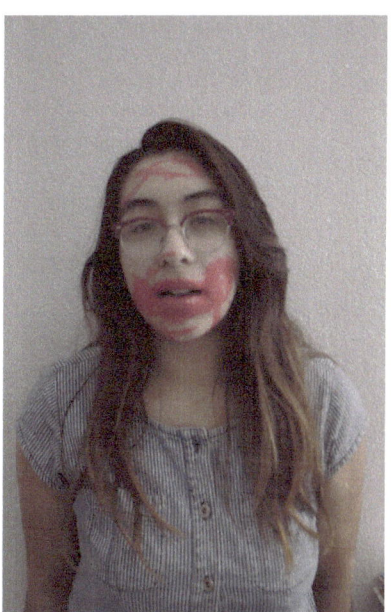

16 NOVEMBER 2017
Self portraits *by Josephine Jael Jimenez*

OUR PEOPLE

BEKAH BADILLA
@bekahbad
bekahbadilla.com

LORRAINE RUMSON
@its.lorraining

BRENDA HERNÁNDEZ JAIMES
@bren_jai
brenjai.com

MELISSA ARELLANO
@melsartpetals

DONYA AVERY
twitter: @skitter_

REBEKAH C. GUERRA
rebekahguerra.com

EVAN BLACK
@evanisthenewblack
evanvblack.com

SADIE KENDRICK
@sadiemkay

JOSEPHINE JAEL JIMENEZ
@josietakestheworld
josietakestheworld.com

YURA SAPI
@vivforthemoment
@advancingartsforward

YOUNG IGNORANTES
@youngignorantes
youngignorantes.com

www.ingramcontent.com/pod-product-compliance
Lightning Source LLC
Chambersburg PA
CBHW040346220526
45473CB00009B/2802